WHAT PEOPLE ARE SAYING ABOUT T. C. STALLINGS

Film Director Alex Kendrick: "He's a brother in Christ, and I am impressed with him on a number of levels. I've been blessed to know him and to have made his friendship."

Film Producer Stephen Kendrick: "He's just a good person. T. C. loves his wife and his kids. He has a powerful testimony and he's using it to impact people's lives."

Comedian Michael Jr.: "Just a cool dude, integrity; he's constantly getting it done. He's pressing toward the mark of the high calling. I love T. C."

Hall of Fame Coach Rick Pitino: "There are so many examples of humility being a catalyst to greater success and happiness. Another is athlete T. C. Stallings."

Former Super Bowl MVP Deion Branch: "T. C. is the big brother I wish I always had growing up. The type of man who always leads by example and does things in life the right way."

NFL Running Back Bilal Powell: "T. C. is a huge inspiration in my life. He showed me how to be a college Christian athlete when I needed it most."

FCA National Director Steve Wigginton: "T. C. speaks from experience and walks his talk. He enthusiastically connects with athletes, coaches, and sports fans of all ages!"

The PURSUIT

T.C. STALLINGS

BroadStreet
P U B L I S H I N G

The PURSUIT

14 WAYS IN 14 DAYS TO PASSIONATELY SEEK GOD'S PURPOSE FOR YOUR LIFE

Published by BroadStreet Publishing Group, LLC
Racine, Wisconsin, USA
www.broadstreetpublishing.com

Cover design by Steve Fryer at www.stevefryer.com
Interior by Katherine Lloyd at www.TheDESKonline.com

Printed in the United States of America

15 16 17 18 19 20 5 4 3 2 1

CONTENTS

FOREWORD

There are often times you meet people in life and walk away thinking, "There's something about that person and I wanna know them." That's what I said when I met T. C. at the premier of *War Room*.

One of the first things T. C. said to me was, "I've been singing your song 'Crazy Faith' over and over and it's stuck in my head."

By the time I was viewing the film at the Atlanta premier, T. C. had already been to more than a dozen screenings. He was well acquainted with everything about the film he starred in. About ninety seconds of my song was in the movie and only the chorus. He had heard it so many times and it was now tattooed on his brain: "Oh God, did I hear you? You really want me to walk up to that mountain and tell it just to move? This is crazy! But it's gonna take crazy faith. So what if it costs me everything? I'm stepping out, I'm taking the leap of crazy faith."

He later went and downloaded the song and posted on Twitter that he was listening to the entire song, weeping because it described his journey *exactly*!

T. C. is a man of faith . . . crazy faith. You're about to read the story of someone who truly follows Christ. It looks crazy to the world around him and often seems crazy to him. He's a man who understands that God has a purpose for his life, even when circumstances scream the opposite.

The principles laid out in this book are absolutely foundational and yet so practical that we can all dive in and get it. No matter where you are in life, this book will strengthen and inspire you! God has as much of an exciting plan and purpose for you and me as He has for T. C. This book will only help you in moving towards it.

John Waller
CCM artist

Prepare

— ☀ —

BEFORE YOU
START DAY ONE

Over the next fourteen days, I am going to share something with you that has radically changed my life, and can do the same to yours too. Together, we are going to rely on some simple truths found in Scripture that should stir something up within you. The Living Word of God will aim to completely change the way you plan to live your life.

I'm not talking about getting saved here, because to even begin to understand what's in these pages one must already know who Jesus is. Before you can experience the incredible journey and the amazing aftermath of this devotional, you have to first be ready to exercise total faith in Scripture and a commitment to following Jesus. Is the Bible the ultimate authority in your life? Decide right now if you really believe everything that the Bible says. If you do, then our two weeks together will definitely result in you becoming extremely passionate about pursuing God's purpose for your life. And trust me from experience, you will love what comes along with doing so.

If you trust God's plan for your life and commit to pursuing it, then your success in accomplishing His plan for your life is guaranteed. Let me say it again: your success in accomplishing God's plan in your life is guaranteed if you will seek Him with your whole heart. How do I know this? Scripture tells me this fact, and God's Word cannot lie. The only thing that can stop the plan of God for your life is you. This is not because you have the actual "power" to stop God; rather, it's because He does not force His will on anyone. Instead, God graciously allows us the freedom to choose—or *not* choose—to pursue His purpose for our lives.

But why would anyone *not* want to pursue God's plan? Well, there can be a lot of reasons for this: doubt, fear, uncertainty, unbelief, and unawareness that God even has a plan for a person's life—just to name a few. I could probably think of more reasons why we neglect God's plans, but instead I would rather focus on the reasons why we *shouldn't* neglect His plan.

My intention in this book is to help you discover why your purpose, which was ordained by God before He created you in your mother's womb, should be your number one pursuit in life. The goal over the next fourteen days is to help you understand the need to become extremely passionate about it.

We'll use fourteen Scriptures, and not one Scripture will be skillfully "twisted" to say what I want it to say. In fact, I'll actually be "untwisting" a few commonly misused verses so that you can understand and apply them properly. Additionally, I am going to share with you a real-life example of how these fourteen Scriptures can impact a Christ follower's life. The example? Me. My own life.

Many people know that I have been blessed with a successful acting career. But what is not known is the way I arrived at this point—a truly incredible story that I am going to share with you. Obviously, from what I have just written and the fact that I'm writing at all, you can preconceive that this story ends well. But it's not the happy ending that matters most; no, it's the *how* that you should focus on. How did I get to where I am today? How did I have so many doors open for me? How did I receive absolutely everything I needed to accomplish all my goals? How did I hear God so clearly? How did

11

I overcome fear? Uncertainty? How did I keep the faith when things appeared to not be in my favor?

This devotional is all about conquering the *how* of your life and completely taking it out of the picture. No more guesswork is needed. If you believe in Scripture, you will develop faith that will become much bigger than the hows of life. What God says about His plans for you will take the place of how they will be accomplished. If you lock into this devotional and take it seriously, you will discover that believing in (and acting on) the upcoming Scriptures will produce the passion needed to successfully pursue your God-given purpose. You are about to read my own story in the next chapter, and how pursuing my purpose took me from complete uncertainty to total victory. No part of my story is an accident, a coincidence, or a case of "good luck." No, what happened to me was ordained by God.

You are God's creation, just like I am. My story of purpose is amazing. But here's the good news: you have your own amazing God-given purpose that is just waiting to be pursued as well. Because of this fact, my hope is that after I tell you the story of pursuing my purpose, and you see what God has done with me, it will inspire you to immediately begin chasing after your own—this devotional will inspire you to do it passionately.

PURSUIT

— ❋ —

THE T. C. STALLINGS STORY

As a child there were two things I cared about the most in life: acting and playing football. I was in plays at both church and school and thought about becoming an actor one day, but football was at the top of my list, what I loved the most, and so I focused on that.

I got a scholarship to the University of Louisville, and had a successful career there. It was always my dream to get to the NFL, and so as a child I always put everything into that goal. Toward the end of my senior year in college, I almost stopped going to school my last semester, barely going to any classes. All of my focus went into preparing for the NFL draft because I felt that was a once-in-a-lifetime opportunity; school would always be there for me. I could always go back to college if I wanted to, but I needed to capitalize on this chance to play professional football.

I had trained hard in football, but I didn't get drafted. I wasn't discouraged because I knew there was still an opportunity to make a team if I went to a personal workout and was impressive. So that was my next plan.

I didn't have a job and wasn't working anywhere, and it took all my resources and savings to travel to different cities and work out for these football teams. Meanwhile, although I should have been working and taking care of my wife and daughter, I thought, "If I put everything into a good showing at these NFL workouts, then the whole money thing will take care of itself."

I wanted my wife to believe in me, which she did. Although she didn't discourage me, she was nervous about how much I was putting into trying to play professional football without a job. But I really believed that I was going to make it to the NFL before we lost all our money. However, we not only lost all our money, but I also still didn't make it to the NFL.

Finally, my wife, Levette, said, "Listen, you need to do something else. I know this has nothing to do with you being a good football player, but this isn't working." Knowing she was right, I reluctantly agreed. I went back to Louisville, finished my last semester of college, and earned my degree. I then decided to give the NFL one final shot. Over the next four years, I excelled in the Arena, Canadian, and European Football leagues—the latter ending with MVP honors. I just *knew* my performance in Europe would get the NFL's attention. It did not. The league was not impressed, and the door remained shut. It was time to fully heed Levette's advice to hang up the cleats permanently. Yet I thought, "Okay, if I'm not going to play NFL football, then what am I going to do?"

One day a friend invited me to go to see a movie called *Fireproof*, which is a Kendrick Brothers' movie about marriage. By the movie's end everyone was in tears, and even I choked up seeing all these men crying and talking about doing better in their marriages. I was blown away by the fact that a simple movie could have so much power and influence in the lives of people. This reminded me how much I loved acting.

I said to my wife, "Wow, if I ever decide to pursue an acting career, I'll have to work with those guys," referring to the Kendrick Brothers. "Just look at what their movies are doing to people," I said. Then I quickly added, "Babe, I don't know how, but some day I'm going to work with the Kendrick Brothers." I knew for sure where my heart was, but the timing wasn't right. There was still the matter of finding a job. Pursuing an acting career would have to wait.

I knew about fitness and personal training, and I knew a lot of people, so I decided to open my own business. Many of my friends became clients, who brought their friends. I was also a strong and active Christian in my church, and I knew from my relationship with Jesus that what I needed to do, regardless of what profession I was in, was to honor God with my profession. "God is blessing me with this training business," I thought. "But how can I honor Him with it?"

So I started putting Scriptures on the walls and added an element of faith to my classes. For example, I had a class called Faith Fit. I gave a free fitness class to anyone who came to a Bible study I was teaching once a week in the gym. I taught Scripture and honored God with the building and language—profanity was not allowed in my gym. Because God blessed the business, I knew that was where He wanted me to be. I flourished financially with a large clientele, and on top of that I honored God with it all. It was a beautiful situation and everyone was happy.

Many months passed while I continued to run things at the gym. Then I heard that the Kendrick Brothers were casting for their next film, *Courageous*, and I got an opportunity to audition for the role of T. J.—and I landed it. Back in '08 when I saw *Fireproof*, I didn't know who the Kendrick Brothers were, but I'd said, "I want to work with them." Two years later the Lord made it happen with my role in *Courageous*.

Courageous came out, did extremely well, and an agent in Los Angeles saw the movie and was really blown away by my performance as T. J. She tracked me down and called me. I was at the studio and answered the phone, and the agent said, "Have you ever thought about coming to LA and making a career for yourself as an actor?"

Of course I'd thought about it, but I couldn't see any way to make it happen. But that's when I thought with my human rationale and said to myself, "Okay, this is nothing but Satan trying to get me to trade honoring God with my facility for coming out to LA to be some kind of superstar."

Not really taking the agent seriously, I said, "Well, that's something I've thought about before, but let me just think about it and I'll get back with you." The agent told me if I came out to California she would love to represent me and thought she could find some work for me. Although I felt flattered I didn't think it would go any further than that phone call.

After I hung up the phone, my wife said, "Who was that?"

"Oh, an agent from Los Angeles," I said.

"Really?"

"Yeah, and she wants me to come out to LA," I said. "Babe, there aren't any roles for me out there—that's nothing but Satan trying to get me unfocused because we're doing so well here and honoring God with our gym."

And I left it alone at that. But Levette said, "Aren't you going to pray about it?"

"Praying about that is like praying about eating," I said. "You know you're supposed to eat so you don't pray about it, you just eat. And I don't need to pray about this because this is not what the Lord wants me to do, it's just something I want to do. The Lord is using me right where He has me."

The problem was that I couldn't get it out of my mind. The more I tried to push it out of my thoughts, the more it stayed. One night I awakened with a migraine. I'd never had one before, but my wife had them all the time. I'd never believed her when she told me how bad they were, but this one was killing me. I woke up Levette, crying, "This headache is squeezing my head and it just won't go away."

"Well, it might be a migraine," she said. "Are you stressed about something? What's wrong?"

"I don't know," I said.

"Are you thinking about the LA stuff?"

"A little bit," I said. "It's on my mind."

"Well, listen, just pray about it and anything else that's on your mind. You've got to relax or it'll just keep you up all night."

So I prayed about the whole LA thing and finally fell asleep. When I woke up the next morning, I said, "I've prayed about it and this seems the only sensible thing to do. Let's weigh the pros and cons of going out to LA."

I started with my pro list, which was very short. It basically consisted of one item: *I could impact the entertainment industry for Jesus.* Period. That's all I had. I couldn't think of another solid reason for the Lord to want me to go LA. I knew many Christians who wanted to be actors and who were willing to put their Christianity on the shelf and do things God wouldn't want them to do usually made it. But it would be a great achievement if I went out there and made it, yet kept myself clean and honored God in the process. Then I could say, "Look, I made it without getting dirty! So you don't have to get dirty either. There's some clean stuff out there. Pursue it, honor God, and go ahead and have your career."

Then I started the con list, which was quite large:

- *I owed personal training sessions.* There were people I trained who paid for their sessions in advance. It wouldn't be right for me to leave while I still owed them training sessions.

- *The lease.* I had a couple of years left on the lease for the gym, the building, and the whole property. When you're paying a couple thousand a month for the lease, they won't just let you out of the contract. I'd be responsible for the rest of the lease, which didn't make financial sense at all.

- *I had over $10,000 worth of equipment that I had bought to run the gym.* What would I do with all of that?

- *I had one particular client who needed to lose over a hundred pounds before he had surgery.* He'd also bought the most sessions, with five or six months left, and he depended on me to get him ready for the surgery. I couldn't just leave him.

- Then there were the bigger things. *Where would we live? How would I make a living with no job?*

There were a lot of negatives and only one positive. So I told my wife, "I have prayed about it. I talked to some of the elders at church, people whom I trust, but this just doesn't make sense. I don't think it's the Lord's will, so there you go."

The agent had given me a deadline of the new year and it was already October, so that only gave me a couple of months to decide. I felt I had done my due diligence by praying, so I went right back to running my gym. But this is where things started to get interesting. One by one the Lord started eliminating the cons from my list, starting with the sessions I owed. When you train people every day, you learn about each other's personal lives, and my clients had heard about the agent calling me. They were excited about the movie *Courageous* and all the attention I was getting. Soon someone said, "So what's the deal with the agent? What are you going to do about that?"

I told them all of the negatives on my con list and the one positive on my pro list. One client said, "I don't know where the Lord's going to lead you, but if the Lord wants you to go out to LA and you don't go because you owe these sessions, maybe you could hire some help." Another said, "Hire some help, do as many sessions as you can, and any you don't finish by the new year, just accept the money as a gift. We want to bless you, and if the Lord's called you to do this, we don't want that to be in the way."

Suddenly that con wasn't much of an issue anymore. So I said, "Thank you and bless you." But there were so many other cons left that I really didn't get too excited.

One of the elders from my church, whom I'd sought wise counsel from, was also one of my best clients. We talked about this situation and he said, "Listen, it's nice that your clients said that they would do that. And if the Lord is leading you to go out there and you decide to take it on, well, I'll buy all of this equipment and make a home gym for myself and all my children."

All I could say was, "Wow!"

"Hopefully that's one of the bigger hurdles out of your way," he said. "Consider that taken care of, so whatever the Lord decides for you to do, just know that the equipment is not in your way anymore."

That was scary but amazing at the same time. But my con list was still long. Then I got a call from the front office that a couple had inquired about our space we were currently leasing. The business park where the gym was had no open buildings, but this couple wanted to start a fitness facility there. It turned out that if I decided to leave, then this couple would assume the lease starting the day I left and I wouldn't owe a thing. I contacted the couple to be sure, and they said, "We'd like to come by and take a look at the place. If we like the setup and the space, when you leave, we'll take it." And that's exactly what they did. They came, looked, and loved it. That was another thing off the list.

Then I saw that my con list wasn't so big anymore. I felt pushed to go to LA and didn't want to go because of my fear of the unknown and because everything was working out. I was counting on my con list to keep me at this gym where I knew what I was doing and things made sense.

I had good reasons for being fearful about making this trip and shutting down the gym. I'd already been irresponsible when I was pursuing football and had let all our money run out. I'd made that mistake once and didn't want to make it again. I had also promised Levette that I would be wise in my choices. And this just didn't seem right, so I called myself extremely responsible and didn't consider making such a drastic move to Los Angeles. I said, "It would be irresponsible to go out there when I don't even know where we'll live."

In 2004, I'd played professionally in arena football, and met and became friends with a kid named Ryan when he joined the team I was on. And I really hit it off with his parents too. The team was in Kentucky, but Ryan and his family lived in California. When they saw that I was a Christian and that Ryan and I were good friends, they asked, "Will you look after Ryan like he's your brother?" I loved the way they took care of Ryan and they were amazing parents, so I invited them over to my house and cooked them a spaghetti dinner one evening. Before the night ended, I told her that I considered Ryan my godbrother. With a smile I said, "I guess that makes you two my godparents." When they went back to California, we stayed in contact through letters.

When this opportunity to go to LA came up, Ryan's mom and I talked about it and I told her what I was going through. She asked, "What are you going to do?"

"Well, there isn't much I can do," I said. "I don't have a place to live in California."

She said, "Well, you know all my kids are gone and we've got four bedrooms. If you need a place to stay while you figure things out, you may live with us. I'll talk to my husband about it, but I'm sure he'll be okay with it." She added, "Pray and see what the Lord wants you to do. But you won't have any bills to worry about."

I was quickly running out of excuses because I now had a place to live. I looked at my con list and felt like the Lord was calling me to go out to LA. But there were two things left on my list: I didn't have a way to make money, and I had that client who had already paid for six more months of sessions. And I couldn't just give him the money back because he was depending on me to get his weight down in time for the surgery. "Okay, there's no way he's going to give up the six months of sessions," I thought to myself, "so it looks like LA is not going to happen."

When my client showed up for his session, I was happy to see him. Before long we began to talk about the whole LA thing. "So what are you going to do?" he asked.

"I'm going to stay right here," I said. "I've got commitments, you being one of them."

"Well, let me ask you something. Have you ever trained anybody online?"

Awhile back, Levette and I had decided to tap into the online experience for those who lived outside our range and couldn't come to the gym, but we needed a guinea pig. So we tried with one lady and helped her lose twenty pounds. On my wall of success, I had a lot of before and after pictures, but she was the only online client we had worked with. I highlighted her as a catalyst to encourage others to let us train them online.

I said, "Yeah, I trained this lady right here."

"You know what?" he said. "That woman is my dentist."

"You're kidding me, right?"

"No, that's my dentist," he replied.

"Well, she can certainly vouch for how well we've done online because I helped her lose twenty pounds."

The client talked to his dentist and she told him we were amazing. He came back and said, "Listen, if you think you can get this weight off me online, I want you to go LA. If I'm the only hurdle left, it's not a problem."

Now I was out of excuses. Every con had been wiped clean except one: *how would I make money?* I had no idea what I'd do for money, but at that point it was clear that God was calling me to take my family to LA. However, He left one thing undone so that I would still have to use some element of faith to make this move.

Levette and I knew it was the Lord telling us to move to Los Angeles. We put our furniture in storage in Louisville, shut down the gym, and packed everything we owned into a minivan. All we had were the clothes on our back, a few important documents, our dog, and our two children. We hit the road, two thousand miles to California, to stay with my godparents.

When my son threw up in the car, I wondered, "What am I doing?" But we got to my godparents in San Bernardino for a trial period. "If nothing happens in ninety days, we go back home," I said. "I don't want to get stuck out here trying to be some superstar and it doesn't work out. We have to know that the Lord wants us here."

We continued praying. With no job, I met with the agent, talked, and decided to see what happened. I wanted to see if she would honor what she had said, which was to look for only clean work to allow me to be me and still honor my faith. So she went to work on it.

Meanwhile, I had nothing to do, which was by God's design. The Lord really strengthened me during this time because with time on my hands and not having found a church home yet, I became familiar with Francis Chan. While I was waiting for an audition, I was listening to Francis Chan sermons and studying Scripture four hours a day. Well, I wasn't getting any work since we were going for only clean stuff, although my agent worked hard.

I really needed to take my mind off of things because I watched my bank account, all the money we came out there with, go down, down, down. Then one day my godparents asked, "Would you lead a Bible study while you're out here?" They knew I was in ministry and that I was familiar with *Not a Fan*, which was the curriculum they wanted to use for the Bible study.

"Okay, I'll do that," I said, relieved because it took my mind off of the fact that no acting work had come in. The *Not a Fan* study has you disclose some personal things about yourself, so everybody in the group, all friends of my godparents, got a chance to hear what I was going through—the whole story. And they thought it was amazing that we stepped out in faith like that.

With only a short time left with the Bible study, my trial period in California was winding down. We were into our last weeks and things were not looking good. I told Levette, "I think we're going to have to go home." Then I told the group, "I think our time is almost up and I don't quite know why the Lord brought me out here. Maybe it was just to lead this Bible study and then go back home, as odd as that may be. But it's time for me to wrap it up."

There was even a chance I wouldn't be able to finish leading the study. Well, the group didn't want me to stop leading the study and prayed through the whole thing with me. They also felt like the Lord wasn't done with me yet in California. Someone asked, "Well, what are the problems?"

"We don't have a place to live and we certainly can't stay with my godparents forever," I said. "And I don't have a job."

At the next session, one of the ladies said, "I own some condos and have one I can put you in, at a price you can afford. We'll figure it all out. But I'm not so sure the Lord is done with you here in California."

"Wow, that's amazing," I said. "But I don't have any furniture."

"Listen, we want to help," someone else said. "If the Lord wants you here, this is what we feel led to do." And just about every person in the group went home and brought back a piece of furniture: beds, TVs, lamps, refrigerators, kitchenware—everything we needed—and furnished that condo so we could stay in it.

"Okay, I might be able to get through a month," I told them, "but then how am I going to pay these bills?" But again, when the Lord does it His way, through other people, you just trust Him and step out in faith. We chose to stay and finish the Bible study, and then we moved to this condo, which was located out in Ontario, California.

Then, out of nowhere, I got requests to speak at different places. Some of them were for Father's Day because I was in *Courageous*; others were just because I was in ministry and they wanted me to speak and teach. I ended up with enough speaking engagements to fund nearly an entire year in California—I didn't need a job to pay for our life. Through all of 2012, I spoke at different conferences and churches, shared my heart and the gospel, and spoke of things I was going through in my walk of faith. And the Lord blessed me for that.

As the speaking engagements started to run out, the

agent I had signed with found me a movie role in a clean, Christian film. So 2013 started off with a movie role, followed by two more roles. Then my agent said, "Hey, have you ever thought about doing modeling? Or what about commercials?"

"No, sure haven't," I told her.

"Listen, while you sit here and wait for movie roles, there's clean work in these other areas too," she said. And she hooked me up with two more agents, a modeling agent and a commercial agent. It's extremely hard to get an agent in the first place, but I ended up with three and didn't have to look for any of them. The acting agent came to me, then she found the modeling agent, and the modeling agent found the commercial agent. I had three agents working for me, and I had the movie role my agent found for me too. Although this was great, none of it was steady work. So I prayed.

One of the pastors from back in Louisville, Kentucky, spoke at a church in California, and told me about how amazing the church was. I said, "Okay, I'm looking for a church." So I visited the church and found out that they needed a youth pastor, which I applied for and got. Now I had the job I needed, three agents, and I was working in the media. But suddenly the church where I worked decided they didn't want a college ministry anymore, that they no longer had the finances for it, and so they canceled it, which left me without a job once again. Just as fast as I had all this stuff, I had lost it.

At the same time, acting had gotten quiet and in the blink of an eye I was back where I started. Yeah, I was in a condo, but the cash flow just stopped and everything got weird. I'd just gotten an A+ evaluation from the church I was working for, then a couple of months later they fired me—canceled the ministry—and I was really floored by this. But before I got a chance to get all bent out of shape and upset, maybe an hour later, Alex Kendrick, from the Kendrick Brothers, called me and said, "I want to officially offer you the lead role in the movie *War Room*."

I was blown away. This movie required a nearly eleven-week commitment, and I couldn't have worked at the church and on this film at the same time. I wouldn't have quit the church to do this film because I feared being jobless again. I loved that ministry, in charge of over a thousand kids, and I felt the Lord had called me there—it was going great. But I truly believe that the Lord got me out of that ministry and freed me up so that I could do *War Room*.

Then I needed a job again, right? Well, right then and there the Lord already had a job waiting for me.

When I got done with *War Room* eleven weeks later, another church called me and offered me the same position that I'd had at the previous church. They were fully aware of my film career and saw that as an asset. Now I was doing film, had agents representing me in nearly every area of the media, and I had a wonderful job as a youth and sports ministry director in Valencia.

It's a beautiful story because it all started when I prayed, "God, what do You want me to do?" When I sought God for His purpose in my life, He just laid it out, and yet He left some things to the imagination so that everything was activated by faith.

Where the pursuit comes in has to do with the reason everything worked out—nothing could stop it because it was all part of my purpose, the reason I was born, the very reason God had made me. Psalm 139:16 says that God has a purpose for everyone's life, and mine was to be exactly where I was; moment by moment God constructed my life with every step. Every moment I went through, as long as I followed Jesus, was a constructed moment used to shape the destiny God had for me. And if I continue to follow that path, I will stay in my purpose doing what God made me to do. No one can stop that, and that's the beauty in it.

When I sat back and thought about everything that

had to go right in order for me to get to the place I was, I realized that God had orchestrated it all. And once I read Psalm 139:16, I realized that every human being has a divine purpose, and that if people would seek their purpose, then something amazing would happen to them. And the cool thing is that if you believe the Scriptures, then you've got to believe Psalm 139:16, that God has a purpose for your life and He's going to walk you right through it the way He did me.

I've found fourteen key Scriptures in the Bible that totally lay this out, fourteen ways to passionately seek God's purpose for your life. This is how I often explain it to people. Some people have a hard time with principles, and God doesn't ask us to follow only principles that are laid out in His Word; rather, He wants us to pursue Him first and foremost. But God still gives us principles in Scripture, and if we pursue them with our whole heart, then we will reap the benefits that they promise.

If you believe in Jesus Christ and His Word, then you have purpose. No matter what bumps and bruises come along on the road to find your purpose—it wasn't all peachy for me—the principles outlined here show you how to deal with them and how God will lead you into your purpose. No one can stop you. These principles will also show you how God will open the necessary doors for you to walk through, while at the same time shutting the other doors you are not supposed to walk through. You'll also see that there will be rough times ahead, even within your purpose. But the different ways God lays out for you to pursue your purpose will help you stay faithful to His plan.

It's such a great thing that every single human being has a purpose, and you've just read about mine. My main motivation behind writing my story and the fourteen ways to passionately seek God's purpose for your life is not to make money or be the greatest author in the world. This is a tool that's going to change lives and point people toward what I know is the most important, most rewarding thing in a person's life—to live out your God-given, God-ordained purpose.

It is my desire that people get up each day, no matter what they're going through, super joyful because they know they're doing exactly what God has created them to do. And it's amazing that Scripture shows you how.

Well, that's my story. What will yours be? I am excited for you. Get ready. These next fourteen days could change everything in your life. Here are fourteen ways in fourteen days to passionately pursue the destiny and purpose that God has created you for.

Day One

DISCOVER
YOUR PURPOSE

You saw me before I was born.
Every day of my life was recorded
in your book. Every moment was
laid out before a single day had passed.

Psalm 139:16

1

—※—

The first of the fourteen Scriptures, Psalm 139:16, sets up everything you are about to experience over the next two weeks. Right away, you are about to be challenged in the very way you view your life. If you fully believe in Scripture, then you can be 100 percent sure that each and every day of your life has a God-ordained purpose attached to it. That alone should fire you up. At the very least, you should be extremely curious about *your* Psalm 139:16—or in other words, God's purpose for your life.

Have you ever actually asked God about His purpose for your life? If you have, then this devotional will help you know how to hear God's response to that question. If you're certain that you have already clearly heard His response but have not acted on it yet, then you are about to be prompted to pursue. If you have heard from the Lord concerning your purpose and begun to obey it, then this devotional will remind you of why you must stay completely committed to it. And, finally, if you have *never* asked God about His purpose for your life, then be sure to take your time in reading this devotional—and stay focused on it for the next fourteen days. I am certain that you will definitely decide to ask Him about His plans for you.

There are some key words and phrases in today's verse that should get your attention immediately. One of them is, "You saw me before I was born." Chew on that for a moment. Before you ever came into existence, God planned out everything that would go into making you, *you*. The person you are and everything about you was by design—God's design—and not simply by accident. After reading that great fact, there is then this jaw-dropping phrase (my goodness, these words have changed everything for me): "Every moment [of my life] was laid out before a single day had passed."

Doesn't that sentence grab your attention? Think about it: tomorrow hasn't come, yet God has already planned, watched, and approved His plans for everybody's tomorrow. And He did all of this before we were born. The Bible declares that God personally designed His plans for your life, inserted them, and then watched it all play out like a movie before you even took shape in the womb. Decide right now if you believe this. If you do, then you must be thinking the same thing I thought after reading Psalm 139:16: "How awesome is this!"

Here is the thought for today concerning the foundational first Scripture to our pursuit. Think of an orange for a moment. An orange starts off as a seed, and that seed can only become one thing—an orange citrus fruit. Why? Because it is prepacked that way. God made orange seeds with a purpose, and He prepacked them with the ingredients to fully accomplish their purpose. That orange seed will burst into a nice orange fruit someday, and when it does it will be doing what God designed it to. It will make orange juice, it will provide vitamin C and other nutrients, or it will be a delicious piece of fruit simply to be eaten.

But what if oranges had decision-making power? What if an orange seed wanted to grow up and burst into a pineapple plant instead? Since this is the orange seed's desire, it then begins to pursue that goal. It drastically decides to move from Florida to Hawaii, because common sense tells it to do so. As a seed itself, it feels the need to be where pineapple seeds best flourish. When it reaches Hawaii, it does everything that the pineapple seeds do. Over time, the pineapple seeds begin bursting into beautiful pineapple plants—exactly what they were designed to do. The orange seed gets excited as it feels itself begin the bursting process too. Only, when it looks in the mirror, it sees that it is a tree bearing nice round oranges. It's not a plant. It's not a pineapple. Instead, it is highly frustrated. Upset. Depressed. Confused as to why things didn't work out like it had planned. So much time went into this plan—and it was all for nothing.

Some people's real lives look much like this. In this example the problem is obvious, right? The orange was made with a prepacked plan yet pursued a totally different outcome. This seed may have absolutely known its purpose but just wanted to be a different kind of fruit. Or maybe it didn't know what it was designed to be and was just following its own desires. The bottom line is that this seed spent too much time, energy, and resources trying to be something it was never designed to be, when all it had to do was verify God's purpose and obey it. If you have never asked God what He wants you to do with your life, then you could be living a life much like the orange in my example.

Psalm 139:16 completely changed my life. It encouraged me to ask God about His ordained plan for my life, because—to me—pursuing any other plan just doesn't make sense. You read my story. I had some very difficult decisions to make. But this Scripture ensured me that if I were to always place God at the center of my decision-making processes, then the outcomes would always be blessed.

God knows your tomorrow. He planned it according to His purposes. Unlike fruit, we do get to decide whether or not we will accept His plan for our tomorrows. In light of Psalm 139:16, and your full belief in Scripture, which path will you pursue from this day forward—His or yours?

QUESTIONS FOR TODAY

- Are your dreams, goals, desires, and plans fueled mainly by what you want to be, or by what God made you to be? What do you think God has made you to be?

- What did God prepack in the seed of your purpose?

- What path do you want to pursue to walk in your purpose? Ask Him today to show you His design for your life.

PRAYER FOR TODAY

God, I thank You for Your love, and that You sent Your Son Jesus to die for my sins, so that through Your grace I can receive Your Holy Spirit and be equipped to live out Your purpose for my life. God, what is my purpose—what is *my* Psalm 139:16? Please show me Your purpose for my life, God; lead me in obeying this purpose, Jesus; empower me to follow this purpose, Holy Spirit. In Jesus' name I pray, amen.

TODAY'S REASON

YOU HAVE A PURPOSE!

Day Two

DON'T STOP
THE PLAN

"For I know the plans I have for you,"
declares the LORD, "plans to prosper you
and not to harm you, plans to give
you a hope and a future."

Jeremiah 29:11, NIV

2

While this next Scripture is one of the more popular Bible verses, it is also one of the most misused. Before we get into that, however, let's focus on how it properly fits into God's purpose for your life. So far we know that God has a purpose and a plan for our lives. Jeremiah 29:11 assures us that this plan of His cannot be stopped by anyone or anything outside of ourselves. We stop God's plan for our lives by never letting it get started, or by quitting it once it does get started. When it comes to Jeremiah 29:11's promise of prosperity (or success of a plan), it is exclusive to God's purpose and plans for our lives, and not applicable to our own ideas.

Don't make the common mistake of following your own goals, dreams, and desires, and then placing the Jeremiah 29:11 tag on it. You'll think you're unstoppable—but you're really not. That's not the intent of this Scripture. In the context of Scripture, the Israelites (God's chosen people) landed in a situation that would have them become slaves for seventy years in Babylon. It was a heavy punishment for disobedience to the Lord. But God did not do this without a victory plan.

During this punishment, God developed a restoration program that, if accepted, would totally refresh the captives. Jeremiah 29:11 was God's promise to the Israelites that if they obeyed His plan while enslaved, then He would indeed prosper them, protect them, and move them toward a much greater tomorrow. But again, this promise of prosperity, safety, and hope was not in relation to any other plan except His own. The Israelites had tried their own way and it landed them in exile.

Think back to my story for a moment. When I first arrived in California and had nothing, I became doubtful of what God was doing in my life, if He was doing anything at all. I seriously had to pray through this rough patch. Jeremiah 29:11 was the promise that helped sooth my worries and calm my fears when I would wake up several mornings with no clue as to how God was going to piece everything together. Some days were uncomfortable for my family as we watched our savings dwindle away with no income to replace it. Times were tough.

Although I wasn't being punished like the Israelites, I still was not fully comfortable with my circumstances. The temptation to try my own plan (like the Israelites) certainly crept into my mind. But Jeremiah 29:11 continuously served as a reminder of the fact that God's ultimate goal is for His plan to prosper. Trying to take the lead would not end well at all. God's plan isn't just the best plan; for the faithful, it's also the only unstoppable one. It's ordained. It's blessed.

Yesterday you faithfully asked God to reveal His purpose for your life. He knew you would do that, and He is certainly preparing an answer for you. Now prepare yourself to courageously respond to His answer by embracing Jeremiah 29:11. Ask God to replace your plans with His plans. And, rest assured that whatever God calls you to do—no matter the circumstances—it will absolutely prosper.

QUESTIONS FOR TODAY

- Do you have a plan for your life? What is it?

- Is that plan designed by God, by someone else, by you, or a mix of these?

- Which do you believe is best for you in the long run: your plan, someone else's, or God's?

PRAYER FOR TODAY

Jesus, I know that God the Father has a plan for my life. As He continues to reveal this plan, please lead me in building up the kind of faith, trust, and courage needed to stay the course no matter the circumstances. Replace my plans with Yours, Lord, so I can avoid a harsh reminder of Your sovereignty. In Your name I pray, amen.

TODAY'S REASONS

You have a purpose
& IT'S GOD-ORDAINED!

Day Three

RENEW YOUR MIND

*Don't copy the behaviors and customs
of this world, but let God transform you into
a new person by changing the way you think.
Then you will be able to know God's will for you,
which is good and pleasing and perfect.*

Romans 12:2

3

Once we become Christ followers, we have to actually follow Christ. We have to go where Jesus is going. We must do what He would do, say what He would say, and think as He would think. How can we have such a superb spiritual mind? It will only come by allowing the Holy Spirit to do the thinking for us. Pursuing God's purpose for your life will be difficult if you approach it with the wrong mindset. It's time to insert Romans 12:2 into your thinking.

When you accepted Christ, you let His Spirit move into your heart and mind. There are usually goals, dreams, and desires already living in these two places, but God wants to clear out both of these areas, removing all the old contents and replacing them with new ones. The key here, however, is that we can't just give Jesus our hearts without giving Him our heads as well. God has to be the main influence on our thinking. If He is not, then we will struggle to accept the patterns of His purposes for us, because our own thinking will think it knows better. Unless you let God change your perspective about *everything*, it will be impossible to passionately pursue your purpose.

We are usually passionate about the things that matter most to us. What is it that matters most to you? If it is different than what matters most to God, then chances are good that He is coming in second place to your first love. His plan for you is next in line behind whatever you think is worth pursuing today.

In my story, my heart was wrapped up in a personal training studio. Interestingly enough, it was being ran with a "Jesus first" mentality. In other words, I actually thought that it was what God had called me to do. But I was eventually able to think as Jesus would have me to think, which allowed me to hear God's call to shut it down. If I was using purely human logic, I would not have thought to shut down a successful business and leave town to go God knows where to do God knows what. But my mind had been renewed, and I was able to know, accept, and passionately pursue God's will for my life—His good, pleasing, perfect will.

My good friend Alex Kendrick once said, "You must be able to recognize the difference between a good idea and a God idea." I love this quote because, with a renewed mind, we can do just that. The Holy Spirit will lead your mind into thinking like Christ, which will help you recognize the God ideas that are attached to His plan for your life.

QUESTIONS FOR TODAY

- Who or what is the main influence on your perspective about your life? Is it the Holy Spirit?

- What are the things that matter most to Jesus? To what degree do they also matter most to you?

- If you were to give God total control of your goals, dreams, desires, and plans—do you believe that you would be pleased with the outcome? What are the risks?

PRAYER FOR TODAY

Father God, I do not want to depend any longer on my own
human logic, or live with a worldly perspective. Transform
my way of thinking. Give me a mind that can recognize Your
voice and obey Your plans. Eliminate the competition, Lord,
which is my old way of seeing things. Help me to understand that Your plans for my life are the most pleasing of
all. In Jesus' name I pray, amen.

TODAY'S REASONS

You have a purpose
& It's God-ordained

& IT'S GOOD, PLEASING, AND PERFECT!

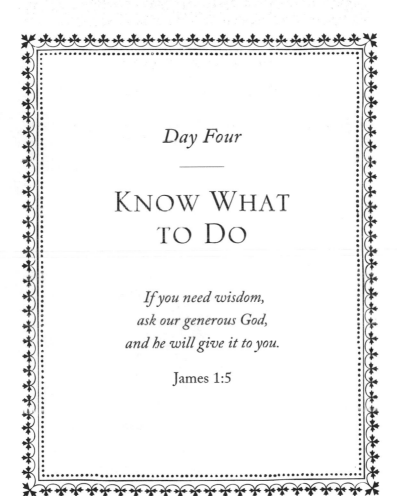

Day Four

KNOW WHAT
TO DO

If you need wisdom,
ask our generous God,
and he will give it to you.

James 1:5

4

Who? What? When? Where? Why? How? Questions. Anytime you and I have to take on a challenge, task, mission, or assignment, we function best when we know exactly what we are getting into (or why we have to get into it, or who will help us get out of it, and so on). We simply do better with challenges when we are confident in our decision making.

For some reason, there is a misconception that Christ followers walk in blind faith. This is not true at all. We may not always know each and every detail when it comes to God's plans for our lives, but we certainly are not kept completely in the dark about it. We could not handle that kind of assignment, and Scripture promises that God would never put things on us that are too much to bear. What God will do, however, is provide you with any wisdom needed to accomplish His divine purposes. It's right here in our next Scripture—James 1:5—and it's pretty straightforward, right? When it comes to your purpose, simply ask God. Why settle for confusion, guessing, or "winging it," when God has graciously offered you access to His wisdom?

You believe you have a purpose, you know that it can't be stopped, and you have a renewed mind, so now you wonder what the first steps to be taken are. You'll wonder where resources will come from. You'll wonder if you are truly obeying His will. These are natural emotional questions. It's tough to handle the uncertainties and unknowns. God knows this, and that is why He has promised to give us the wisdom that we need to make the right moves in life. We just need to ask Him.

It is possible to know exactly what to do when it comes to pursuing your purpose. You can make all the right decisions if you passionately attempt to seek God's direction and obey Him. I'm not talking about living a perfect, mistake-free life. Mistakes always happen. But they need to happen while following Jesus and your purpose so that He can quickly get you back on track. When your mistakes take you down the wrong road of life, you can rely on the wisdom of God to get you back on the correct one.

Just as a GPS recalculates and reroutes us when we make a wrong turn, the Holy Spirit is ready to do the same concerning our wrong turns in life. We simply need to repent for the error, then seek His wisdom concerning our next move. If confusion concerning God's purpose for you ever sets in, just know that you do not have to let it stay, because you are never without access to God's wisdom. There is no excuse or reason for any Christ followers to feel as though they have no clue of what to do. James 1:5 takes all the guesswork out of pursuing your purpose in life. I'll say it again…just ask.

I asked God if I should move to California. He said yes. I asked how I would make a living, and He said, "Leave that up to Me; meanwhile, lead a Bible study for eight weeks." I could go on and on with how God fed me continual wisdom during this time of my life. And it totally makes sense why He would do this. God wants us to succeed in pursuing His purpose for us, so why would He hold back from us the wisdom needed to prevail? He doesn't. He'll tell you everything you need to know so that you'll know exactly what to do and when to do it.

Today, before you get going, think about the fact that the all-knowing God has promised to share His wisdom with you. As you pursue your divine, unstoppable purpose, remember James 1:5 and walk confidently with the Lord. Keep in mind that verses 6–8 warn us against doubting God and His wisdom. If you doubt Him, that's a deal breaker. The Bible says that doubters get nothing (verse 7). So let James 1:5 encourage you today. All your prayers concerning the wisdom you will need for decisions you must make will be generously answered by our God. What a blessing that is indeed.

QUESTIONS FOR TODAY

- Have you been asking God for His wisdom concerning the many decisions you make each day? If not, then why not?

- What does James 1:5 say about this? Will you do so now?

PRAYER FOR TODAY

Father God, I humbly admit that I have no idea what tomorrow holds. I believe You have a plan for me, and I want to pursue it while avoiding wrong turns and improper decisions. Please let Your wisdom always be the source of my planning, and may I never doubt Your power. In Jesus' name I pray, amen.

TODAY'S REASONS

You have a purpose
& It's God-ordained
& It's good, pleasing, and perfect
& IT'S GUIDED BY GOD'S WISDOM!

Day Five

DO GOD'S WILL

Not everyone who calls out to me,
"Lord! Lord!" will enter the Kingdom
of Heaven. Only those who actually do
the will of my Father in Heaven will enter.

Matthew 7:21

5

This Scripture is the biggest motivator for pursuing God's will in your life, for your place in heaven is at stake. Read it again. How much clearer can Jesus be than what He outlines here for us in Matthew 7:21? If you do not pursue His Father's will, you will not see heaven. Are you motivated yet to pursue God's plan for your life?

This is not a scare tactic, but rather a truth tactic, because we believe that the Bible is the true, perfect, infallible Word of the Living God, written by those He called and inspired. So if the Bible says that God is the creator of your life's purpose (Psalm 139:16), then obviously it is His will for you to fulfill that purpose. That being said, can you possibly be comfortable with not knowing God's will for your life after reading the words of Jesus in Matthew 7:21?

If we read on in Matthew 7:22–23, Jesus says that there will be many people seeking credit for some of the "good things" that they did in Jesus' name, but Jesus will say, "I never knew you." This is an important point that cannot be missed—the fact that the "goodness" did not matter in the end. Remember when Jesus called Peter when he was fishing? In obedience, Peter stopped fishing when Jesus said to him, "Follow Me." Is there anything wrong with fishing? No. But what would have made fishing wrong for Peter was if, after Jesus told him to stop fishing and follow Him, Peter decided to keep fishing instead. Peter wasn't hurting anyone. He may have even had plans to give most of his fish to the poor—in Jesus' name. Sounds like a good idea, right? But it's not. It is actually disobedient. It is telling Jesus that you think your plans are better than His Father's plans.

According to Matthew 7, this is a dangerous mindset to have—no matter how good you think your plan is. If your good idea doesn't include allowing Christ to lead you in obeying God's will, then you will fall victim to Matthew 7:21–23. Can you imagine living your whole life according to your own seemingly "good" agenda, feeling good about your accomplishments, regularly receiving praise from others, and being told what a "good" person you are, only to hear Jesus say to you in the end, "Away from Me, I never knew you," all because you ignored God's will?

Those who become passionate about their purpose

should not fear Matthew 7:21. If you have been focusing and praying through this devotional so far, then your passion should be stirring. Up until this point, you have renewed your mind and asked God to reveal His will for your life. Now Jesus can properly develop a loving relationship with you, and lead you in pursuing God's will for your life.

Keep this in mind today: success comes to many people for many reasons. Many people like to give credit to God whenever they are successful. This always looks and sounds good, but our Scripture for today reminds us that God may not always be behind everyone's success. Jesus is not in the lead of every good idea. He's in the lead of His Father's ideas, and God will only honor the lives of those who seek this will above their own.

You cannot let success be the single determining factor for the choices that you make concerning life, since God is not always behind everything that appears successful. Allow God's will—His purpose for you—to be the driving force for what you decide to do today, and every day. This way you can live your life in peace, with nothing to fear. And when you do finally meet Jesus, He will know exactly who you are.

QUESTIONS FOR TODAY

- When you read Matthew 7:21–23, what does this mean to you?

- In what ways are you "doing the will of the Father"?

- What will Jesus say to you in the end?

PRAYER FOR TODAY

Father God, my prayer today is simple. I do not want to be shocked at the end of my life and have heaven's door shut on me. So I ask You, as humbly as I know how, to please keep me aware of Your will. Help me to stay firmly behind Your Son Jesus. Holy Spirit, empower me to do what God made me to do. I pray this in Jesus' name, amen.

TODAY'S REASONS

You have a purpose & It's God-ordained
& It's good, pleasing, and perfect
& It's guided by God's wisdom
& IT'S GOD'S WILL AND MUST BE DONE!

Day Six

ASK HIM FOR EVERYTHING YOU NEED

You can ask for anything in my name,
and I will do it, so that the Son
can bring glory to the Father.
Yes, ask me for anything and I will do it!

John 14:13–14

6

—※—

From the mouth of the Savior comes this great promise. When Jesus says things like this, we need to put it in its proper context and decide whether or not we believe it. This verse gives it to you straight: you will never lack what you need to accomplish God's purpose for your life. And don't you just love that Jesus says it twice, as if He knew we might doubt what we just read? "You can ask Me for anything, and I will do it…. Yes, ask Me for anything and I will do it." Thank You, Jesus.

Keep in mind that for this promise to take effect, however, we must be doing what God has called us to do. The goal of Christ is for His Father to be glorified, for His will to be done on earth as it is in heaven. If that's the goal of your day, then Jesus promises to do whatever is necessary to accomplish it in your life. We were made to give God glory, and if we are simply willing to do what we were made to do, then we can expect to receive anything we need to succeed. Within your own life and purpose, insert this promise. If your God-given purpose requires _____ (fill in the blank), and you ask Him for it, then you will receive it. Whatever you need to accomplish God's plan, that He will do.

The great thing about John 14:13–14 is that this is Jesus talking. Do you trust Jesus? Then you can be confident that you will never be without the tools, resources, or breakthroughs needed to prosper while following Him. When I made the trek to Hollywood to pursue acting professionally, I had no job and no home. Within a year, however, I had a new home, a full time job with benefits, and three entertainment industry agents. Evidently, these were some of the necessities that Jesus knew I needed in order to accomplish God's plans for my life. All I did was what John 14:13–14 said to do: I asked Jesus to give me whatever I needed to accomplish God's purpose. Then I obeyed Him as best I could in all areas of my life. Piece by piece, and in His timing, He blessed me with everything I needed (and removed anything I did not need). Glory be to Jesus Christ, who always keeps His promises.

Today, as you continue to pursue God's will, remember that there is no need to spend any time at all wondering if you will have what you need to succeed. The answer, according to Jesus, is a guaranteed yes. How can anyone in Christ not be fired up about this?

QUESTIONS FOR TODAY

- Do you believe that Jesus will supply all your needs as you pursue God's will?

- What are the needs that you have right now?

PRAYER FOR TODAY

Jesus, thank You. You are my provider, and You are my source for whatever is needed to obey Your Word. As You continue to prepare me to accomplish God's purposes, I thank You in advance for giving me anything I need to succeed. In Your name I pray, amen.

TODAY'S REASONS

You have a purpose **&** It's God-ordained
& It's good, pleasing, and perfect
& It's guided by God's wisdom
& It's God's will and must be done
& IT'S FULLY RESOURCED BY JESUS!

Day Seven

BE READY
FOR EVERY ATTACK

*The thief comes only to steal and
kill and destroy; I have come that they
may have life, and have it to the full.*

John 10:10, NIV

7

---※---

The Bible promises that anyone who wishes to live a godly life will endure some form of hardship (2 Timothy 3:12). Interestingly enough, this is one of the ways that we identify with Christ. That brings us to John 10:10. Whenever Satan decides to launch an attack against you, this is a good indicator that you are on the right path. When you decide to pursue God's purposes for your life, Satan will attack and try to insert his own agenda. We do not need to spend a bunch of time on this fact. Instead, we need to focus on why Satan is so interested in stopping you.

Satan is doomed to destruction, and there is nothing he can do to change that. What he can do is work as hard as possible to take people with him. So why target you? Why not someone else? Listen to me closely. If Satan is attacking you, you are either seriously close to getting on the right track with God or you are already on the right track with Him and making a huge impact for Christ. Either situation makes you a threat to Satan's agenda.

Those who are passionate about fulfilling their God-given purpose will be attacked. You're a solid Christ follower who is passionate about your purpose. So yes, Satan will attack you. But it's okay because Scripture also reminds us in John 10:10 that Satan's agenda of destruction must contend with the agenda of Jesus: "I have come that they may have life, and have it to the full." Jesus will always be your protector as you boldly live out your attack-worthy life of purpose.

Keep this in mind: Satan can't stop you because he can't stop God. Through Jesus, your God-given purpose will always move forward—regardless of a satanic attack against it. I have definitely experienced Satan's attacks in my line of work. He's constantly trying to tempt me to compromise my values when it comes to film and TV. I've learned to not even tolerate it. I've learned to battle temptation by praying, calling on the name of Jesus, and continuing to pursue what I know is right. Resist the Devil, and he will flee from you. You can do this exact same thing. The very next time that Satan attacks you, pray. Call on the name of Jesus. The Son of God crushing Satan is built into the purpose of all Christ followers.

QUESTIONS FOR TODAY

- What kind of threat are you to Satan?

- In what ways are you living a life "worth attacking" due to your spiritual impact for Jesus on others?

PRAYER FOR TODAY

Father, help me to understand that it is truly an honor anytime we suffer due to following Your Son Jesus. Give me the strength and courage needed to push through the trials that may come while obeying Your plan for my life. Help me remember that the battle against Satan is Yours, not mine, and is a battle that he cannot win. I pray this in Jesus' name, amen.

TODAY'S REASONS

You have a purpose **&** It's God-ordained
& It's good, pleasing, and perfect
& It's guided by God's wisdom **&**
It's God's will and must be done
& It's fully resourced by Jesus

& SATAN CAN'T STOP IT!

Day Eight

PRAY CONTINUALLY

Never stop praying.

1 Thessalonians 5:17

8

---※---

What seems like a no-brainer to Christians can sometimes be one of the most overlooked aspects of our faith. In this case, I'm talking about prayer. Right away, it must be understood that prayer is not optional. In fact, it is crucial if we are to fulfill the purpose for which God created us.

We speak to God through prayer, show our faith through prayer, and build a relationship with God through prayer. Show me a person who doesn't pray and I promise you that this person unfortunately is not living out their God-given purpose. You can feel as though you are highly gifted and strong spiritually, with tremendous respect and reverence for God, which may be true, but that doesn't mean He is leading and guiding your every step. Only prayer can assure that.

Imagine you are in the military and you have been called to war. You have great respect and admiration for your commander. Maybe this commander has led you to the battle lines. You have been given combat gear, weapons, camouflage, and a walkie-talkie for communication. The commander has the war plan, and plans to guide you to—and through—the entire operation. Communication will obviously be key. Soon, the time comes to go into the battle. You charge the field in pure determination, arriving with guns, knives, bombs—everything you need—except your walkie-talkie. You left your only source of communication with the commander back at the base. You have all the ammunition in the world but no clue what to do with all of it. Hard to win a battle this way, right?

In the same way, Christians can't win spiritual battles without prayer. Think of God as the Commander, and prayer as your walkie-talkie. Each day that you take on the spiritual battles of life without communicating with the Commander, you are choosing to fight without guidance from the only one guaranteed to lead you into victory.

"Never stop praying." To obey this Scripture, it is important to understand that it does not mean that when you start praying, you can never stop talking. The concept behind "praying continually" is the idea that Christ followers must not simply live life, but rather live life—*every* aspect of it—through prayer. Psalm 139:16

says that God laid your life out "moment by moment." This is why we must pray through all situations, seeking the Holy Spirit's direction to ensure that we walk within these ordained moments. And since we are called to battle Satan on the front lines of spiritual warfare, this is no time to lose communication with God. What a shame it would be to rush into battle without prayer, which is the one weapon and resource that matters most.

Refuse to allow a poor prayer life to be a part of your relationship with Jesus from this day forward. Your ability to carry out your purpose depends on how committed you are to talking to Jesus—daily—about every aspect of your life. Prayer is one of the primary ways we pursue our God-given purpose.

QUESTIONS FOR TODAY

- What grade would you give your prayer life: A, B, C, D, or F? Why?

- Is that a grade you are willing to live with? How can you get your grade up?

PRAYER FOR TODAY

Father, I cannot accomplish Your purpose without a commitment to prayer. I never want to go through life leaving You out of the picture. I realize that prayer is my greatest weapon in the spiritual battles of life. Thank You for the privilege of prayer. Help me to never stop praying. In Jesus' name I pray, amen.

TODAY'S REASONS

You have a purpose & It's God-ordained
& It's good, pleasing, and perfect
& It's guided by God's wisdom
& It's God's will and must be done
& It's fully resourced by Jesus
& Satan can't stop it

& IT'S POWERED BY PRAYER!

Day Nine

MAKE DISCIPLES

*Therefore, go and make disciples of
all nations, baptizing them in the name
of the Father and the Son and the Holy Spirit.
Teach these new disciples to obey all the com-
mands I have given you. And be sure of this:
I am with you always,
even to the end of the age.*

Matthew 28.19–20

9

———— ☼ ————

We know this Scripture as the Great Commission and recognize it as part of every Christian's purpose. This is Jesus simply telling us to go out into the world and share Him with others. No matter what God has called you to do concerning your individual purpose, Matthew 28:19–20 speaks to your collective Christian purpose. Collectively, all Christians have a few things in common when it comes to God's purposes: we must all love God, we must all love people, and we must all go and make disciples. A part of every Christ follower's God-given purpose is helping others to realize theirs.

Today, commit to allowing the Holy Spirit to lead you toward opportunities to introduce someone to Jesus. There is no need to force the issue. Pray for a God-led opportunity, and when it arises take it. Sometimes this will need to be done with words, other times with actions. Sometimes you will be in the process of making a disciple and you won't even know it. How? Because someone will be watching you one day, someone who is interested in Jesus, and your lifestyle will become the way that this person first forms an opinion about Him.

How you approach this command to make disciples is a good indicator of how close you are to Jesus. How so? Because He promises to "be with you always, even until the end of the age" if you obey His command to make disciples. Do you really want Jesus to be with you in all that you do? Then pursue your purpose passionately, which will lead to making disciples. And don't miss this: Jesus not only says, "Tell others about Me," but He also says, "Then teach them about Me." That's what we call true discipleship.

I knew that God would always be with me when I decided to become an actor, because He knew that I understood that discipleship needed to always be a top priority. If you ever doubt whether or not you are truly fulfilling your purpose, just ask yourself this question: "How many people have I introduced to, and taught about, Jesus?" The way this question gets answered should dictate your next move. If your answer is none, or not very many, then don't waste time drenched in guilt. Just repent, ask for guidance, and plan to go and make disciples—starting today.

QUESTIONS FOR TODAY

- How many people have you led to Christ? Who do you know personally that you would like to see come to know Christ?

- How many people are being discipled by you (meaning, you are helping them to follow Christ closer)? Who might you reach out to, offering to help them grow in Christ?

PRAYER FOR TODAY

Jesus, I realize that making disciples is a command, not an option. By the power of Your Spirit, help me have the wisdom, courage, and power to share Your name with anyone You point me to. Help me lead them into a proper relationship with You as a true follower. In Your name I pray, amen.

TODAY'S REASONS

You have a purpose & It's God-ordained & It's good, pleasing, and perfect & It's guided by God's wisdom & It's God's will and must be done & It's fully resourced through Jesus & Satan can't stop it & It's powered by prayer

& IT CREATES CHRIST FOLLOWERS!

Day Ten

GLORIFY GOD WITH HOW YOU LIVE

*Let your good deeds shine out for all to see,
so that everyone will praise
your heavenly Father.*

Matthew 5:16

10

Today's reason for becoming passionate about your purpose is one of the best there is. Read Matthew 5:16 again. What's one of the ways that God gets glorified here on earth? By what we do in our actions. Jesus is the light, and this light lives on the inside of those who have accepted Him as Savior and Lord. Through those who allow this light to shine, good deeds happen, and God is glorified as a result. For this reason, obedience to the Word of God matters. Following Jesus wholeheartedly matters. What you do in your day-to-day life matters.

God does not accept "selective" Christian living (people treating the Bible like a spiritual buffet). These type of people love to pick and choose which Scriptures they want to obey. Or there are some who live with the idea that they can do whatever they want with their lives as long as they remember to give God credit when good things happen to them. Neither of these choices work. In fact, here is exactly what Jesus says about such people:

"These people honor me with their lips, but their hearts are far from me" (Matthew 15:8, NIV).

One of the biggest reasons many people doubt Christianity is because of what some of us choose to do with our lives. We sometimes allow too much sin to creep in, while using the "nobody's perfect" cliché as a crutch. When the world sees this, they come to the conclusion that Christians are fake, judgmental hypocrites. Once they feel this way, many never come to Christ, not because of *Him* but because of *us*.

Our imperfections are supposed to serve as opportunities for Jesus to show His transforming power to the world in which we live. As God consistently removes sin from our lives through the power of His Spirit, many will witness these victories and some will eagerly want what you have. While our good deeds don't bring us salvation, they do bring God the glory He deserves. The bottom line is that unless you allow Jesus to refine you daily, you will never be able to fully live out God's purpose for your life.

Jesus said, "Anyone who believes in me will do the things I have been doing" (John 14:12). Is this your goal, to do what Jesus did? If not, then it must be. This Scripture declares that if we truly believe in Jesus, we will model our lives after the one He lived. In this way, our light shines for all to see, which is a big part of God's purpose for allowing you to live.

My own life changed dramatically once I realized that what I do as a Christian matters. Respect for Jesus, combined with a passion for my God-given purpose, has shaped everything I do concerning my life and career. Once God saw this shift in my perspective, He began to use me to impact the lives of others for His glory. He wants to do the same for you.

If you haven't already, you must make it a goal to live your life in such a way that God is consistently glorified through it. Literally, just ask the Holy Spirit to lead you into living a life that daily brings God tremendous glory. What you do with your life matters.

QUESTIONS FOR TODAY

- How is God receiving glory from others because of the way you live your life?

- In what ways can people see your life as a biblical example of how Jesus can strengthen, transform, and refine an imperfect person for His glory?

PRAYER FOR TODAY

Jesus, I now know that what I do with my life reflects how well I know You. What I do can cause people to glorify our heavenly Father or contribute to the reason that many reject You. Please help me to not settle for being an imperfect sinner, but to allow You to refine me and cause my imperfections to be a means to God's glory, as I allow the Holy Spirit to change me more and more each day. In Your name I pray, amen.

TODAY'S REASONS

You have a purpose & It's God-ordained & It's good, pleasing, and perfect & It's guided by God's wisdom & It's God's will and must be done & It's fully resourced through Jesus & Satan can't stop it & It's powered by prayer & It creates Christ followers

& IT BRINGS GOD GLORY!

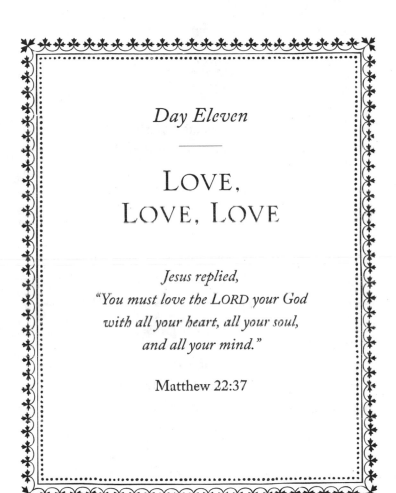

Day Eleven

LOVE, LOVE, LOVE

Jesus replied,
"You must love the LORD your God
with all your heart, all your soul,
and all your mind."

Matthew 22:37

11

Love. Forget about passionately pursuing your purpose if you do not know how to love well. This is another must-have quality for anyone who desires to do God's will with his or her life. God must teach you how to love all people in His way.

Today, we need to look at Scripture and understand how serious God is about loving properly. Read Matthew 22:37. You will hear Jesus say that we are to love God with all of our heart, soul, mind, and strength. After all, there's really nothing left to give—so He's asking us to empty the tank when it comes to love. It is impossible for us to obey this command on our own, but don't worry, this is why we have the Holy Spirit. He will do the loving through you, but you must be willing to consistently let Him do it. To love like this is a command, not an option.

While Matthew 22:37 is our main Scripture, here are two more supplemental Scriptures that we also need to look at concerning love. In John 14:15, Jesus said, "If you love me, obey my commandments." Jesus says that if we truly love Him, then we will do what He says—plain and simple. We can't claim to have a love for God while not striving to obey Him in all that He has revealed to us.

Then Paul wrote in 1 Corinthians 13:1–3:

> If I could speak all the languages of earth and of angels, but didn't love others, I would only be a noisy gong or a clanging cymbal. If I had the gift of prophecy, and if I understood all of God's secret plans and possessed all knowledge, and if I had such faith that I could move mountains, but didn't love others, I would be nothing. If I gave everything I have to the poor and even sacrificed my body, I could boast about it; but if I didn't love others, I would have gained nothing.

Talk about straightforward. This Scripture basically says that you can do whatever you want for God, but if the love of Christ Jesus is not in you or in the reason behind what you are doing, then it has no value. You don't have anything. And notice that I did not say "you must have love." No, I said that you must have "the love of Christ Jesus." There is a big difference there. You must allow Jesus to teach you how to love His way, because the human definition of love is not even close to how God defines it.

Think about the way you love God and people. If you need a change of heart, ask for it right now. If you do not know for a fact that God has changed the way you love, then make that the top priority above all else. Study every Scripture on "love" that you can find. Pray for Jesus to train you in the art of love. If you don't handle this love situation first, then—as Scripture says—you have nothing. That "nothing" includes the ability to passionately pursue God's purpose for your life. It's impossible to do it without Christlike love.

QUESTIONS FOR TODAY

- In what ways are you following Jesus' example of loving God and others?

- What do you want your life to look like in the future as you learn to love in a Christlike manner?

PRAYER FOR TODAY

Jesus, I realize that Your command is for me to love You
with all my heart, soul, mind, and strength. Please, Lord,
teach me how to do this. Help me to see others the way that
You see them so that I can love others the way that You do.
In Your name I pray, amen.

TODAY'S REASONS

You have a purpose & It's God-ordained
& It's good, pleasing, and perfect & It's
guided by God's wisdom & It's God's will
and must be done & It's fully resourced
through Jesus & Satan can't stop it &
It's powered by prayer & It creates Christ
followers & It brings God glory

& IT IMPROVES THE WAY YOU LOVE!

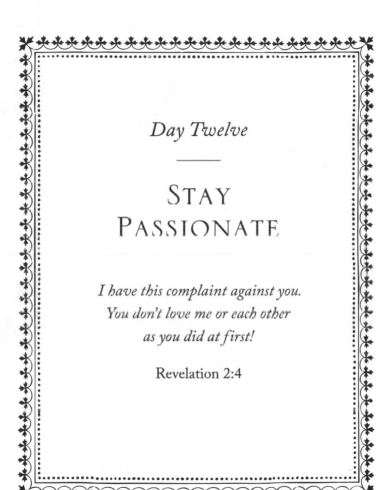

Day Twelve

———

STAY PASSIONATE

I have this complaint against you.
You don't love me or each other
as you did at first!

Revelation 2:4

12

What can derail a person while living out their God-given purpose? There are many things, but one of them is losing passion. When it comes to walking with Jesus each day, you must stay passionate about it and never begin only going through the motions. This is why the tagline on this devotional is not simply, "Pursuing Your God-Given Purpose." No. We have to do it passionately, with intensity, with fervency.

A marriage can get into trouble when either the husband or wife loses passion; likewise, Christians get into trouble when they allow themselves to become less passionate about God. It's that classic case of "getting bored with doing right." It'll start to feel as though everyone else is having all the fun. This is when Satan and sinful temptation knock at the door and are usually let in.

In the beginning of living out our purpose, we are on fire. Satan lays low, knowing that "now is not a good time" to attack. We are much too full of the Spirit for him to tempt us. What Satan is counting on, however, is our "growing weary in doing good." Our gradual loss of passion. It is at this point that we become much less disciplined than normal, and so we begin to compromise. We play with gray areas. We procrastinate with our purpose. This is when Satan attacks. He hopes to do a lot of damage while we are less passionate than normal.

More important than what Satan can do is what Scripture says Jesus will do. In Revelation 2:2–5, Jesus basically praises a church for a lot of the good things that it does. But He had a problem with their passion. They stopped loving Him as they once did, and they stopped obeying Him with passion. They were doing good things, but they had obviously started slacking and allowed sin to creep in. Jesus warns them that if they do not bring back the passion that they once had, He would not allow them to continue to fulfill their purpose of shining for Him.

When it comes to your purpose, you must do it with passion, or God may not allow you to do it at all. This is especially true for those of us whose lack of passion leads to lack of control over sin. God can't allow us to freely sin and still represent Him to the world. Personally, I love representing Jesus with my career. I love that He has called me to do it. But I know that if I do not do this passionately (so that I don't run the risk of misrepresenting Him), He can shut it all down in a heartbeat.

Whenever you feel as though you are losing any passion, desire, or energy while pursuing your purpose, be sure to stop immediately and pray, asking God to restore the passion like you had when you first started serving Him. Your passion for your purpose is like fuel. The Holy Spirit has to fill you up again. Take time to refuel that passion whenever you need to, because your purpose can't run on empty. Stay passionate to keep moving.

QUESTIONS FOR TODAY

- Do you feel as though you live an energized Christian life, still in love with Jesus as you were at first, or do you feel less passionate than you used to be? Why?

- What can you do to refuel your passion for Jesus?

PRAYER FOR TODAY

Jesus, by the power of Your Holy Spirit, keep me infused
with the desire, passion, and energy needed to pursue God's
purpose for my life. Help me to passionately keep in step
with You and the Spirit. In Your name I pray, amen.

TODAY'S REASONS

You have a purpose & It's God-ordained
& It's good, pleasing, and perfect & It's
guided by God's wisdom & It's God's will
and must be done & It's fully resourced
through Jesus & Satan can't stop it &
It's powered by prayer & It creates Christ
followers & It brings God glory
& It improves the way you love

& IT KEEPS YOU USEABLE!

Day Thirteen

STAY CONNECTED

Yes, I am the vine; you are the branches.
Those who remain in me, and I in them,
will produce much fruit.
For apart from me you can do nothing.

John 15:5

13

Read John 15:5—slowly and focused—again. Apart from Jesus, you can do absolutely nothing. This Scripture requires some serious humility to fully embrace it. But I cannot stress how true it is. I would not be anywhere near my purpose if it had not been for Jesus, and I have learned to accept that I must stay connected to Him if I truly desire to be spiritually productive. You must also embrace this truth if you want to passionately pursue your God-given purpose.

Passionately pursuing your purpose is great, but if you ever think that you can pursue it without staying connected to Jesus then you're wrong. You can try, but you will fail. Jesus says that it can't be done. He alone is the source of everything you need to do God's will. Without staying connected to Him, there is absolutely nothing you can do for God.

What does it mean to "stay connected"? Staying connected means having true, consistent daily prayer. Staying connected means reading and studying Scripture on a daily basis. Staying connected means obeying Him wholeheartedly in all that He has spoken to us. Staying connected means disconnecting from the ways of the world and being proud that you did so. It's spiritually holding hands with Jesus as He walks you through your life. When you choose to live this way, you are choosing a life of victory.

Take a moment to humble yourself and be reminded of who your purpose in life serves, and who it's all about. It serves God and it's all about Jesus. God has a purpose for your life that runs through the blood of Jesus. For this reason, you must stay connected to Christ. Without Him, you have no purpose to be passionate about. There is nothing you can do for God apart from His Son. Never forget this as you strive to live for God. You'll be tempted at times to go into situations ahead of Jesus. Don't! Let that temptation drive you back to John 15:5. Remind yourself that apart from Jesus you will fail, but if you stay connected to Jesus, you have the promise of successfully living out your God-given purpose. You will bear much fruit as you abide in Him.

QUESTIONS FOR TODAY

- What have you attempted to accomplish but it just didn't work? Did Jesus lead you to do this?

- What do you need to do to remain properly connected to Jesus so that you can properly follow Him?

PRAYER FOR TODAY

Jesus, please get in front of my life. Please stay there. Never allow my mind to think I can live life apart from You. Help me to stay connected to You in everything and in every moment of my life. In Your name I pray, amen.

TODAY'S REASONS

You have a purpose & It's God-ordained & It's good, pleasing, and perfect & It's guided by God's wisdom & It's God's will and must be done & It's fully resourced through Jesus & Satan can't stop it & It's powered by prayer & It creates Christ followers & It brings God glory & It improves the way you love & It keeps you useable

& IT CONNECTS YOU TO CHRIST!

Day Fourteen

DO IT NOW

Look here, you who say, "Today or tomorrow we are going to a certain town and will stay there a year. We will do business there and make a profit." How do you know what your life will be like tomorrow? Your life is like the morning fog—it's here a little while, then it's gone. What you ought to say is, "If the Lord wants us to, we will live and do this or that." Otherwise you are boasting about your own pretentious plans, and all such boasting is evil.

Remember, it is sin to know what you ought to do and then not do it.

James 4:13–17

14

—※—

This last devotional day focuses solely on the above Scripture, our final reason for becoming passionate about our purpose—James 4:13–17. Please read it again carefully. Here are a few important reminders for today as we move forward following God's will for our life.

Verse 14 is a reminder of Psalm 139:16. You don't know "your tomorrow," but God does. This verse is also a reminder that whether it's by Christ's return, death, or old age, life is simply not long; rather, it is quite short. Verse 15 is a reminder that in light of verse 14 you should acknowledge that God makes the plans, not you. In other words, pursue His purpose for your life, not your own plans and dreams and desires. On the other hand, verse 16 is a reminder that it is a sin to ignore God's purpose for your life while pursuing your own agenda, while verse 17 is a reminder that it is a sin to procrastinate when it comes to obeying God's call on your life. (Do not wait!)

Here is a photo to remind you that you never know what day of life will be your last.

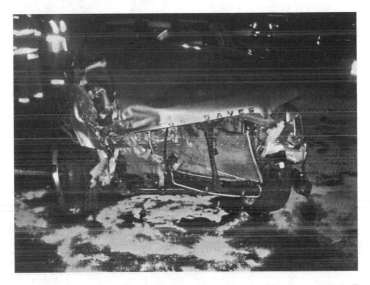

Yes, the truck in the photo was mine. Back in 2010, I was headed to do something I had been doing every Monday, Wednesday, and Friday morning at 6:00 a.m. for the last several months—going to play basketball at church.

The night before this terrible accident, I did what I always did: laid out my gym bag and filled it with my gear—my shorts, shoes, and mouthpiece. On the morning of the accident, I did what I always did, which was stop at the gas station in front of the church to buy an energy drink. I had the same plan on my mind as always: chug down the drink and hurry to the gym before teams were picked. I had everything planned as usual. What I did not plan for, however, was the high-speed van that would run through my truck. I never saw it coming, and pulled right out in front of it. I always thank God that it was a van and not an eighteen-wheeler. I could have died that day.

I am not telling you this to scare you. Fear is the wrong reason to pursue your purpose. The truth of the matter is that I did not truly understand how short life could be until I nearly lost mine. Near-death experiences can (and usually do) cause us to think a bit harder about life and reevaluate what we are doing with our time on earth.

On the day of this crash, once I settled down, I had a life-changing thought. I asked myself, "Since becoming a Christ follower, am I sure that I have been living out God's purpose for my life?" My answer was no. I realized that I had never really asked God what my purpose was. I was trying to live for Christ, but I was doing it my way, only doing what I thought was best. I thought about what I needed to do differently. The list was long: be a better husband, father, and Christian; go on more mission trips, study Scripture more, pray more—to name just a few.

The crash changed my perspective. I was already a

Christian and I was obeying Christ, but I was not consulting Him about my purpose. Fast forward several years, and I am now in love with my God-given purpose.

What you have been reading over the last several days has been a collection of Scriptures that were most influential once I began seeking God for His plans concerning my life. Each Scripture helped me understand the importance of discovering why I still have breath in my lungs. I had been a Christian for several years leading up to the crash, and had been licensed in ministry for seven years, but I was not passionately pursuing my purpose with urgency. I depended on tomorrow way too much and often put things off for another time. But when you think with an eternal mindset, understanding that life is short and each day is not promised, the necessary urgency gets created.

This brings us to our last reason—urgency. Do not put off pursuing your God-given purpose—not even for one day. There is no time to waste. And like James 4:17 says, if you know that you need to do something for Jesus and you do not do it, you sin. So don't put off for tomorrow what you know you need to do today.

You now have fourteen good reasons to passionately pursue your purpose. Remember, all Scripture in the Bible is God-breathed and useful in preparing us to do what He has called us to do (2 Timothy 3:16–17). The fourteen verses that I have shared with you were (and still remain) instrumental in helping me develop the passion that I have today, and I pray that you allow the truth of God's Word to do the same for you. God has created you with a divine destiny and wonderful purpose. Seek it passionately today.

QUESTIONS FOR TODAY

- How does knowing that you cannot predict the day that you will die or when Christ will return affect how you approach each day?

- Are you putting off for tomorrow something that God is asking you to do now? If so, what?

PRAYER FOR TODAY

Lord Jesus, I humbly ask that You take full control of my life, creating a spiritual sense of urgency that will not allow me to procrastinate concerning Your plans for me. Please create a passion in me that cares most about God's purpose for my life above all else. Give me a mind, heart, and spirit that causes Your will to be the focus of my days. In Your name I pray, amen.

TODAY'S REASONS

You have a purpose & It's God-ordained
& It's good, pleasing, and perfect & It's
guided by God's wisdom & It's God's will
and must be done & It's fully resourced
through Jesus & Satan can't stop it & It's
powered by prayer & It creates Christ followers & It brings God glory & It improves
the way you love & It keeps you useable
& It connects you to Christ

& YOU MUST PURSUE IT NOW!

—

A passionate Christ follower who is living out
his or her God-given purpose. And if you passionately pursue your God-given purpose,
then nothing can stop His plans for you.

THE WRAP-UP

As you continue to read God's Word, there are many more things Scripture will reveal to you that will create even more passion toward your God-given purpose. Because of the truth of Scripture, these fourteen reasons have hopefully gotten things started in your heart and spirit. My prayer is that these last two weeks have lit a fire inside of you that will never die out. May you always be passionate about your purpose, and lead others into doing the same.

MY PRAYER FOR YOU

May God's ordained unstoppable plan for your life, through your obedience to it and the leadership of Jesus, and through the power of the Holy Spirit, accomplish the purpose for which it was created—to lead people to Jesus and bring God glory. In the name of Jesus I pray, amen.

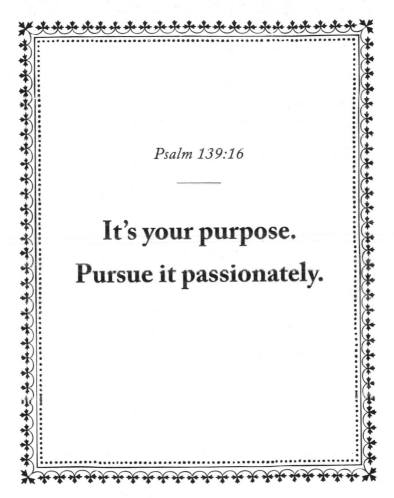

Psalm 139:16

———

It's your purpose.

Pursue it passionately.

Knowing that the one and only all-powerful God of the universe has designed an unstoppable plan for your life should cause you to chase after this plan with everything you have.

—T. C. Stallings

WWW.TCSTALLINGS.COM